MW01139905

Temptation

....

Fighting the Urge

Timothy S. Lane

New
Growth
Press
www.newgrowthpress.com

New Growth Press, Greensboro, NC 27404
Copyright © 2010 by Christian Counseling & Educational Foundation. All rights reserved. Published 2010.

Typesetting: Robin Black, www.blackbirdcreative.biz

ISBN-10: 1-935273-16-7
ISBN-13: 978-1-935273-16-5

Library of Congress Cataloging-in-Publication Data

Lane, Timothy S.
   Temptation : fighting the urge / Timothy S. Lane.
      p. cm.
   Includes bibliographical references and index.
   ISBN-13: 978-1-935273-16-5 (alk. paper)
   ISBN-10: 1-935273-16-7 (alk. paper)
   1. Temptation. I. Title.
   BT725.L36 2010
   241'.3—dc22
   2010002964

Printed in Canada

21 20 19 18 17 16 15 14   11 12 13 14 15

I can resist anything but temptation.

Oscar Wilde

Bob prefers order and control over chaos and interruptions. He's been a Christian for years, but he still fights the temptation to be impatient with his children when their needs disrupt his life.

Sally finds solace in a strong drink. She stays sober for weeks, and then suddenly gives in to the temptation to drink all weekend.

John struggles with pornography. He is single and travels for work. When he is alone on a business trip, he sometimes watches sexually explicit shows on the hotel pay-per-view channels.

Kristen is a hard worker. Everyone in the office knows this, but they also know that several years ago she almost lost her marriage because of her work habits. She's trying to balance work and home, but she still fights the temptation to achieve and to be recognized for those achievements.[1]

Bob, Sally, John, and Kristen lead very different lives, but they are all struggling with the same thing— giving in to temptation. Can you identity with them? How many times have you tried to change a behavior or attitude only to find yourself doing the same thing again? Do these phrases sound familiar? "There I go again!" "I've had this struggle for years, and I just can't seem to win." Or "I do okay for awhile, but then I get caught in the same old sin."

Each of us faces some kind of temptation every day. And, even though our temptations are different, our struggles are similar. We all have daily battles with temptation that stretch into monthly and yearly wars. Can those daily battles against your particular temptations be won? God, in his Word, says, "Yes," and this minibook will help you to take a close look at what God says about how to win your battle with temptation. Learning how to handle your everyday skirmishes with temptation will prepare you for the times when your struggle with temptation becomes particularly intense. But you can't win a war against an enemy you don't understand. So let's begin by learning about temptations: where they come from and why they are so hard to resist. You might be surprised by what you find out about you and your temptations.

Where Do Our Temptations Come From?

It's easy to think our temptations come from our circumstances: Bob's tempted to be grumpy because his children are noisy. Sally drinks because she's in a difficult marriage. John indulges in pornography because his job takes him on the road. Kristen spends too much time at work because her boss is demanding. If temptation comes from our circumstances, then we can deal with temptation simply by changing our circumstances.

But is this really true? Think about your life. If you change your circumstances, your particular temptation might change, but you will still struggle to do what's right. If Bob responds to irritating people with anger, then, even when his children are grown, he will still be tempted to get angry at the irritating people in his life.

It's true that our external circumstances bring temptation into our lives, but God says in the book of James that we succumb to temptation because of what's inside of us (what we want, desire, don't want, fear, etc), not from what's outside of us (our circumstances). When James talks about hard circumstances he uses a Greek word that can be translated either as *test, trial,* or *trap.* This is what he says:

> Consider it pure joy, my brothers, whenever you
> face *trials* of many kinds, because you know that
> the testing of your faith develops perseverance...
> Blessed is the man who perseveres under *trial*,
> because when he has stood the *test*, he will
> receive the crown of life that God has promised
> to those who love him.
>
> (James 1:2–3, 12, emphasis mine)

Here James is describing one's external circumstances as a trial or test that God allows for the purpose of growing us in grace. But the translation of the Greek word changes in verses 13–15 to *tempt:*

> When *tempted*, no one should say, "God is
> *tempting* me." For God cannot be *tempted* by

evil, nor does he *tempt* anyone; but each one
is *tempted* when, by his own evil desire, he is
dragged away and enticed. Then, after desire has
conceived, it gives birth to sin; and sin, when it
is full-grown, gives birth to death.

(James 1:13–15, emphasis mine)

James is saying that God sends circumstances into
our lives to test us, so we will grow in grace. But then he
says that God never designs those circumstances in order
to trap us. Any circumstance is either a *test* that will help
us grow or a *trap* that leads to failure and sin. One pastor
puts it this way,

Thus temptation is like a knife. It may be useful
to cut the meat, or to cut the throat of a man.
It may be a man's food or poison, his exercise
or destruction.[2]

What makes the difference? It's the inner condition
of the person in the midst of the circumstance. Notice
what James says is the ultimate cause of temptation that

leads to sin: "but each one is *tempted* when, *by his own evil desire*, he is dragged away and enticed" (James 1:14, emphasis mine). No external circumstance makes you sin. You sin because what you want leads you into sin.

We Are Tempted in Bad Times and Good Times

Your circumstances are the context in which you experience temptation. In James 1 there are two verses that are crucial for helping us be alert to temptation in all kinds of situations.

> The brother in humble circumstances ought to
> take pride in his high position. But the one who
> is rich should take pride in his low position.
> (James 1:9–10)

These verses highlight two different contexts for temptation. James uses riches and poverty as the example, but he is referring to something more general. Not only does temptation arise in difficulty (poverty), but also in seasons of blessing (prosperity). You might think that the only time we are susceptible to temptation is when things are difficult. But we can be tempted in both good times and bad. Temptations arise when there are certain conditions:

1. *Conditions that make obedience challenging*—like poverty, persecution, difficult children, a troubled marriage, to name a few. Any circumstance that makes it difficult to obey and easy to rationalize doing the wrong thing is a context for temptation. For example, having a demanding boss that threatens to fire you could be a condition that makes it tempting to lie and cover up any mistakes you make; or being married to a critical spouse could be a condition that tempts you to have an extramarital affair.

2. *Conditions that make it easy to sin*—like prosperity, obedient children, a good marriage, to name just a few. Pride and spiritual indifference are two temptations that often arise when life is good. For example, if you have obedient children, you

might be tempted to be proud and to look down on other parents who have unruly children; or if you become financially successful, you might be tempted to forget God and make money and possessions the center of your life.

So pay attention to your circumstances. Are you in a season of difficulty or blessing? Be vigilant. Either condition provides ample opportunity to temptation and sin.

What Are the Elements of Temptation?

There are three basic elements to any temptation. The Bible calls these three elements the world, the flesh, and the devil. We have already discussed the first two (our circumstances and how our desires interact with our circumstances), but Satan also plays a part in our struggle with temptation. Let's look briefly at how the three elements of temptation interact together.

1. *External difficulties and blessings (the world):*
   This element includes our past, our physiological

strengths and weaknesses, and our relationships. These things don't determine our behavior, but they do make us more susceptible to responding in a certain way. For example: If you grew up in a verbally abusive home and experienced very little love in your family, then that external pressure might make you more susceptible to anger, bitterness, and despair. Suppose, on the other hand, you grew up in a strong, loving family with a lot of affirmation. This external reality, which is a great blessing, could still lead someone to be ungrateful, demanding, and proud. Of course, we don't all respond in the same way to our external circumstances. Your response to your circumstances also depends on the two other elements to temptation.

2. *Internal motivations, cravings, fears, and desires (the flesh):* This is the element of temptation that James describes as "evil desires" (James 1:14). Jesus calls this the "overflow of [the] heart" (Luke 6:43–45). How does our internal motivation interact with

our external circumstances? Let's suppose that the approval of others is so important to you that you would do almost anything to get it. When you are criticized, you feel distraught and unhappy. Your desire for approval could lead you to react in a number of ways. You might lash out in anger, becoming depressed and isolated, or you might work even harder to gain others' approval. The external criticism was the occasion for how you responded, but according to James 1:13–14, what caused your particular response was the internal condition of your heart. Understanding this truth should encourage you as you fight temptation. Why? Because although external circumstances can't always be changed, God promises that he can and will change our hearts.

3. *External spiritual opposition (the devil):* The apostle Peter says, "Be self-controlled and alert. Your enemy the devil prowls around like a roaring lion looking for someone to devour" (1 Peter 5:8). Jesus was

conscious of the schemes of the devil throughout his ministry, and you should also be aware of your enemy and his schemes. The way the devil works is quite simple. He uses the external world and your sinful inclinations to trap you into sin. Then he accuses you of being a hopeless case. Thankfully, the Spirit says something completely different. The Spirit says, "If we confess our sins, he is faithful and just and will forgive us our sins and purify us from all unrighteousness." And, "You, dear children, are from God and have overcome them, because the one who is in you is greater than the one who is in the world" (1 John 1:9; 4:4). Although the devil is a powerful enemy, he is no match for what God can do as we depend on him for faith and protection (Ephesians 6:10–18).

Understanding all the elements of temptation is critical in helping you fight temptation. Rather than just focusing on your external situation, you can understand the complex nature of temptation and are better able to see the role your own desires and Satan have in the temptations you are facing.

The Stages of Temptation

Another important truth about your temptations is that they don't just appear in your life—they come in stages. Bob didn't wake up one morning and suddenly become a control freak. Sally didn't become an alcoholic overnight. John wasn't consumed with pornography the first time he saw a suggestive picture. Kristen wasn't a workaholic her first day on the job. Look again at James 1:13–15, and notice how James describes the different stages of temptation.

1. *The first stage of temptation is seduction* ("he is dragged away and enticed"). Temptation begins with your desire life. You want something more than you want Christ. You believe that you need something in addition to Christ in order to be happy, satisfied, or okay. It could be anything— someone's approval, something you want to buy, a

pleasure you want to experience, a job, or a family. Your temptation might be something obviously sinful (like pornography), but often we are tempted to put even a good thing at the center of our lives instead of God. For example, if you are a father who wants his child to love and obey God, that is a good desire. But when that desire becomes more important to you than God, it will lead you to do ungodly things. You might use sinful anger or guilt to get your child to obey. And if you succeed, you might be tempted to think you and your child are better than other parents and their children. Your greatest opportunity to triumph over sin is at this beginning stage of temptation. Ask the Holy Spirit to help you see what you are drawn to besides Christ.

2. *The second stage of temptation is conception* ("after desire has conceived"). When temptation moves to this stage, the initial desire is lodged deep in your heart. At this stage of temptation, what you want is becoming more important to you than

your relationship with God. Perhaps you want to buy something you don't have the money for. During this stage you start planning how you can get it. Or maybe you are convinced that you have to be in a certain relationship to be happy. So you start dreaming about how to move that relationship forward. Perhaps you are longing for the relief a chemical might supply. Your craving for relief or comfort is eclipsing your relationship with Christ. Even though you haven't committed the actual behavioral sin at this point, your desires are sinful. It is a serious thing to lust after something (whether it is a new outfit, a relationship, or a chemical high). Still, there is hope! Now is the time to fight your desires, instead of giving in to a sinful action.

3. *The final stage of temptation is birth* ("it gives birth to sin; and sin, when it is full–grown, gives birth to death"). The end result of your desire for something besides Christ is being caught in full-blown

sin, both in attitude and action. Notice that the birth that's produced is really a death. This is one more step toward being mastered by something other than Christ. As serious as this is, there is still hope. Life is not over when you fall into sin.

At any time during these different stages of temptation, you can run to Christ, repent of your sin, and learn from your failure how to stand against temptation instead of giving in to it. God can change your heart so that, instead of a particular sin dominating your life, bit by bit you will be tempted by it less and less. The rest of this minibook will give you practical ways to resist temptation and depend on Jesus for the help you need.

Practical Strategies for Change

Fighting temptation begins by noticing what's happening underneath the surface of your life every time you give in to temptation. Here is an important truth to remember as you struggle with temptation:

> *You don't behave your way into sinful responses, so you can't behave your way out of sinful responses. You worship your way into sinful responses, so you must worship your way out of sinful responses.*

You might be thinking, "What does worship have to do with my struggle with temptation?" In reality, worship has everything to do with our temptations because whatever we worship (whatever is most important to us) changes our behavior.

You have probably seen this principle at work in your own life, without even noticing it. For example, have you ever been in the middle of an argument when your phone rings? What happens to your behavior when you pick up the phone and say hello? Most likely you answer the phone with a calm voice. What changed your behavior? Was it the person on the other end of the phone who changed you? No, it was a change of heart— a change in what you wanted and desired the most. You were arguing because someone had gotten in the way of what you wanted (perhaps your desire to be treated a certain way, or a desire to be left alone, or a desire that they act a certain way), but with the ringing of the phone, what you want changes. Now you want someone to think well of you. Your object of desire (worship) has changed from winning an argument to your reputation and that changes your behavior.

When you sin you *are* breaking God's rules, but your sin is much more serious than that. In that moment of sin, something else is more attractive to you than God and his love for you. You are worshiping something or someone besides God. It could be personal comfort, success, control, power, achievement, being right, pleasure—anything you desire more than God. Fight against temptation by admitting that your behavior is wrong, but don't stop there. Admit to God that your behavior is the result of forgetting your identity in Christ and finding your identity in what you believe you need besides him.

Don't be discouraged when you notice what's captured your heart instead of Jesus' care and commitment to you. Name what it is, confess your sin to God, and ask for forgiveness. Remember, "If we confess our sins, he is faithful and just to forgive us our sins and to cleanse us from all unrighteousness" (1 John 1:9, ESV).

Remind yourself that, even though you have loved something more than God, Jesus is still completely committed to you. He lived, died, was raised, and sent his Spirit for you. Right now he is praying for you, and one day he will come to rescue you completely. Make every effort to remember who you are in Christ. You are not a slave to sin; instead, you belong to Christ (Romans 6; Galatians 2:20). He is far more committed to you than you are to yourself. He is far more satisfying and attractive than anything else in this world.

On the basis of these truths, begin to have a conversation with your Redeemer. Interact with him as you bring your sins before him. You can go to him and tell him all about your struggles. He understands what it is like to live in a broken world as a human, and he will give you mercy and grace as you ask (Hebrews 4:14–16). Christian change only happens in relationship with God. So getting to know Jesus as your friend, brother, and Savior will change your desire life and give you the power to resist temptation.

Fight Temptation by Knowing Yourself

Now you can apply these truths about worship to the *particular* sinful behavior that you struggle with. Take some time to think about what it is that you want more than Jesus that leads you into sinful behavior. The four people we introduced at the beginning are falling into temptation because they are living for something besides Christ:

- Bob lets his desire for comfort crowd out his love for Christ. When he does that, he becomes impatient and angry with those who threaten his comfort.
- Sally is in a difficult marriage, and she desires peace. Drinking is her way of catching a break from the pressures of her life.
- John lets pleasure and the adoration of another person take the place of his love for Christ. Indulging in pornography gives him the pleasure that he desires, and it also lets him imagine that other women are adoring him.
- Kristen lives for success and achievement. When she gets these, she feels like somebody. What her coworkers think of her matters more to her than what Christ thinks of her as his child.

What about you? What is it that makes your life worth living?

- When are you most content?
- When do you get angry?

- What are you getting that you don't want?
- What are you not getting that you do want?

As you answer these questions, look over your life, day by day, and you will begin to see the patterns that cause you to stray from your love for Christ. Since your heart is the issue, begin by assessing what's happening in your heart when you are tempted.

Become Aware of Typical Circumstances

One of the most helpful ways to fight temptation is to understand what are the times and places where you are typically tempted. This means taking note of what is going on in your world when you are tempted. So ask yourself what kinds of conditions lead you in the direction of temptation and sin:

- Certain places?
- Around certain people?
- Is it seasonal?
- Does the time of day matter?
- When you are discouraged?

I know I am more likely to be tempted to live for comfort after a long day at work. When I am tired and worn down, it's easy for me to sin. I am tempted to think that I deserve to rest with minimal interruptions. So I am vulnerable to the temptation to be impatient with my wife and children.

Don't Minimize the Mundane Nature of the Fight

When fighting small or large sins and struggles, we often focus on the actual moment of giving in to temptation and sin. But sins don't spring out of nowhere. A one-night stand doesn't happen in a vacuum. It is always preceded by days, months, possibly years of temptation. If the moment of temptation and sin is "high noon," then there are hours that preceded that moment. A fall into sin develops over time. So don't downplay the daily battle that is a part of the Christian life. Every day a war is raging for your heart and affections. In any given hour of your day, there are many things that can take your gaze off of Christ. Be vigilant in the little moments of your life. This is where the battle will be won or lost. Your goal should be to cultivate a normal, regular, moment-by-moment awareness of your relationship with God and your need for his grace and power.

So live wide awake. It is easy for daily life with all of its seemingly unimportant details and decisions to lull you to sleep. You start living casually because you only see the big tragedies or big decisions as the places where you need to be spiritually alert. But if you aren't vigilant moment-by-moment, then, when the big things come your way, you will be caught by surprise. Think of it this way: You can't be a couch potato for years, and then run a marathon. Since your heart, muscles, and lungs weren't conditioned daily, you will collapse a few blocks into the run! The same principle applies to temptation. It's important to see every moment of life as an arena for keeping in spiritual shape as you deal with little irritations and small successes. Then, when the big things come your way, you will be ready (Romans 13:11–14; Hebrews 12:1–3).

Bring Your Sin into the Light of Day

What do you need to do daily that will keep you in good spiritual shape? A good place to start is with bringing your struggle into the open. Sin grows most freely and swiftly in secret, so keeping your temptations and sins hidden is very dangerous. Your willingness to tell other wise Christians about your struggle shows how serious you are about changing (and your unwillingness to talk to others is an indication that you aren't as serious about changing as you might think).

So find another Christian (or several) and ask them to talk with you, pray with you, and help you to be accountable. God doesn't expect us to change on our own. He has designed his church as a place for you to gain hope, help, and strength. Christians who grow the most are the ones who spend time with other Christians. James 5:16 says to "confess your sins to one another" (ESV). God tells us in Hebrews 3:12–14 and 10:19–25 that the body of Christ is the primary place where we receive help and encouragement to fight against sin and live the Christian life. Don't try to tackle the power of sin all by yourself; use the encouragement of others who love Jesus to help you.

Treat the Bible Like Good Food

Another way to fight temptation is to go to God in his Word. In Psalm 119, the psalmist describes how we should approach the Bible. Over and over, he talks about how the Scriptures are like good food—sweeter even than honey (Psalm 119:103). Do God's words delight and strengthen you every day? If you don't know how to use the Bible to get to know your heavenly Father and his love for you, then it won't be much help to you when you are tempted. Start by asking the Spirit to speak to you through the Bible. As you hear God's voice in his Word, you will grow to love it. Ask the Spirit to use the Bible to connect you to your God. Then, in the midst of temptation, the Spirit will be able to use God's own words to remind you who God is, how much he loves you, and how pleasing him is the best thing—way better than whatever sin you are tempted to commit.

Make a commitment to memorize Bible passages that will help you see Christ more clearly. Look for passages that highlight the blessings of obedience as well as the warnings of disobedience. A great passage to start memorizing is Philippians 2:1–11. Paul reminds us of who we are in Christ and calls us to treat others the same way Jesus has treated us. Instead of making others the place where you find acceptance, comfort, and love, this passage teaches that Christ came to deal with a deeper need than human approval. He came so you might receive and live in the reality of his forgiveness and comfort.

Meditating on Scripture means more than memorizing. It also includes persistent prayer in light of the Scripture. God gave you the Bible to help you know him, and prayer is how that relationship becomes real and meaningful in the moment of temptation. Find tools that will help you discover passages that address your particular temptation and that also speak about God's freely offered love and forgiveness. Over time those passages will begin to own you as they point you to Christ and bring you into a deeper relationship with him.

Be Prepared to Take Drastic Action

You must also be willing to take drastic measures to avoid close contact with temptation. Jesus says in Matthew 5:27–30 that if your eye offends you, pluck it out. Jesus is not telling you to literally pluck your eye out. He is exaggerating to make the point that you must be willing to take extreme measures to avoid situations where you know you will be tempted. Some people get software for their computers to block certain sites. Some people who travel for work have set up a system of accountability with friends who call them throughout their trip. Be as creative as you need to be to grow in grace! Although your circumstances don't cause you to sin, there are places and things you should avoid because you are prone to desire, love, and want them more than Christ. For example, if you know that you are prone to worship yourself by looking at pornography, it is a good thing to set up structures that guard you from having easy access to suggestive pictures.

Don't Lose Heart If Your Desires Don't Change Quickly

God can and will change your desire life. But that change usually happens slowly, over time. There are times when change happens instantaneously, but that is the exception, not the rule. Paul, in Romans 7, admitted that as a Christian he struggled with being obedient. This is the same Paul who had an amazing conversion on the road to Damascus (Acts 9). But even though he had a dramatic change in his life, he continued to struggle with loving and obeying Christ throughout the rest of his life.

Take a moment and read through Romans 7. Be encouraged by Paul's honest description of the ongoing fight you are in. Imitate Paul by sharing your struggles with others so they can help you. Paul didn't struggle alone. His struggles moved him closer to Christ and closer to other believers. The Christian life is lived in community with God and other Christians. If your struggle with temptation is moving you in these two directions, God will change your desires. You might not notice this from one day to the next, but over the years you will be able to look back and be thankful for the work the Spirit has done in you.

The Spirit is the one who is able to fix our eyes on Jesus instead of on our own desires and/or failings. Paul closes Romans 7 by saying, "What a wretched man I am! Who will rescue me from this body of death? Thanks be to God—through Jesus Christ our Lord!" (Romans 7:24–25). Knowing Jesus better will lead you to live a vigilant, hopeful life as you face temptations every day. Genuine fighting of temptation happens as you take your eyes off yourself and readjust your gaze on Jesus and what he *has* done and *is* doing in your behalf. For Bob that means recognizing that his self-defined need for comfort is not his real need; instead, his real need is for forgiveness and the power to love God and others. This is the dynamic that will enable Bob, Sally, John, Kristen and you to move forward in the fight against temptation and sin.

Above all else, don't lose hope. After all, you and your sin are no match for God's goodness, power, holiness, and grace! The encouraging promise of the gospel is that God moved toward you before you wanted a relationship with him. Paul says, "For while we were still weak, at the right time Christ died for the ungodly" (Romans 5:6, ESV). This is your comfort and your motivation in your daily fight against temptation. Don't lose heart; look to Jesus, the author and finisher of your faith (Hebrews 12:2).

Endnotes

1 All names are fictitious and personal details have been changed.

2 John Owen, *Temptation: Resisted and Repulsed* (Carlisle, PA: Banner of Truth, 2007), p. 3.